*"The great artists of the world are never Puritans,
and seldom even ordinarily respectable."*

—H. L. MENCKEN (A WRITER)

St. Luke, the patron saint of artists

Lives of the Artists

of the

MASTERPIECES, MESSES
(and What the Neighbors Thought)

WRITTEN BY Kathleen Krull

ILLUSTRATED BY Kathryn Hewitt

Houghton Mifflin Harcourt

Boston New York

For information about permission to reproduce selections from this book, write to Permissions,
Houghton Mifflin Harcourt Publishing Company, 215 Park Avenue South, New York, New York 10003.

The Library of Congress has catalogued the hardcover edition as follows:
Krull, Kathleen.
Lives of the artists: masterpieces, messes (and what the neighbors thought)/written by Kathleen Krull;
illustrated by Kathryn Hewitt.
p. cm.
Includes bibliographical references and index.
1. Artist—Biography—Juvenile literature. 2. Artists and community—Juvenile literature. [1. Artists.]
I. Hewitt, Kathryn, ill. II. Title.
N42.K78 1995
709'.2'2—dc20

ISBN: 978-0-15-200103-2 hardcover
ISBN: 978-0-544-25223-3 paperback

Manufactured in China
SCP 10 9 8 7 6 5 4 3 2 1
4500463195

The illustrations in this book were done in watercolor and colored pencil on watercolor paper.
The display type was hand lettered by Judythe Sieck.
The text type was set in Goudy.

For Jacqui and Melanie, two terrific artists

—K.K.

For David, my patron of the arts,

and for Chris Madans, archangel of art history

—K.H.

CONTENTS

$\mathscr{I}$NTRODUCTION

CAN IT BE dangerous to be neighbor to an artist? Neighbors of artists have risked ear damage—from enduring the same song blaring one hundred times in a row (Warhol) or early-morning violin serenades issuing from the bathroom (Matisse). Even worse, neighbors are apt to end up *in* a work of art, displayed for posterity as models, willing or not. Those close to artists have been portrayed with a pig's snout (Cassatt), shocked to find themselves in the midst of great historical or biblical events (Rembrandt), and immortalized in the ultimate pose—as corpses (Leonardo da Vinci).

Yet the element of danger cuts both ways. Neighbors have indeed dodged paintings hurled from an artist's window (Chagall). But artists have had stones thrown at their windows by neighbors protesting a turbulent lifestyle (Picasso). Neighbors have been mystified by weird shadows radiating from an artist's darkened rooms (Michelangelo), and at their most superstitious, they've suspected an artist of witchcraft (O'Keeffe). Savvy neighbors might have sneered to realize that the more money an artist spends, the less he has (Dali), but savvy artists have thwarted inquisitiveness by buying adjoining lots to keep neighbors at a distance (Kahlo and Rivera). Neighbors have been known to protect artists from Nazi persecution (Kollwitz), but they've also banded together to run an artist out of town (Van Gogh). And in terms of sheer quantity, perhaps no one can claim as many neighbors as restless artists, especially when they move themselves and their families a total of ninety-three times (Hokusai).

Much careful research later, it turns out that perhaps no cultural figures have inspired more gossip than artists. (Reputations can be so singular that some artists, such as Rembrandt, need only a single name to identify them.) *Why* this occurs is a subject of controversy. Are artists—and their works—simply more noticeable?

In any case, the twenty artists in this book had interesting lives and interesting neighbors. Here, guided by their patron saint, are their stories, full of masterpieces and messes, offered now as a way to know them—and their artworks.

—*Kathleen Krull*

LEONARDO DA VINCI

BORN IN ANCHIANO, ITALY, 1452
DIED NEAR AMBOISE, FRANCE, 1519

Italian painter and sculptor, genius of the Renaissance,
famous for the Mona Lisa, The Last Supper,
and encyclopedic notebooks

FOR SOMEONE WHO may have accomplished more than any other man in history, little is known about Leonardo da Vinci—except that his curiosity was unique. We know that his father (a lawyer) never married his mother (a peasant), which created lifelong legal and emotional problems for him. As a child he lived mostly with his father and had four stepmothers in all, but it's thought that an uncle who lived nearby nurtured Leonardo's powerful drive to learn.

Leonardo was apprenticed as a youth to the artist Andrea del Verrocchio (a legitimate son would never have been forced to learn a trade, especially one so disreputable as art). One day when Leonardo painted an angel—he was known to draw the faces of angels better than anyone—the older man reportedly threw down his brushes in jealous admiration and swore that he would never paint again. Still, Leonardo always felt at home at Verrocchio's and in times of stress liked to return for visits.

"It is easy to become a universal man," a young Leonardo wrote—and he somehow made it seem so. He never stopped his studies, working on countless projects, or at least starting them. In addition to artist, he could have easily become a city planner, architect, inventor, engineer, physician, musician, anthropologist, botanist, or astronomer. "I question" were the words he wrote most frequently in the elaborate notebooks he kept. He questioned practically everything: What causes tickling? Why are stars invisible during the day? What would it be like to walk on water? Would a fly make a different sound if you put honey on its wings?

Every night Leonardo investigated anatomy in a way few others could have tolerated: he dissected corpses. His sources for bodies were either prisons where criminals had been executed or hospitals for the homeless. He could befriend a one hundred-year-old man one night and make drawings of the corpse the next.

Many of his neighbors were likely to have been scared of Leonardo. He was so mysterious — with his secret autopsies (officially banned by the Catholic Church), his scientific experiments (rumored to be some type of evil magic), and his desire for privacy (his notes were written backward so others couldn't read them). He was even left-handed, believed in those days to be a sure sign of the devil at work.

In others, Leonardo inspired devotion. He was strong, healthy, and handsome, with a carefully brushed and curled beard. His rose-colored robes were short, unlike the long robes of most men, and he was always impeccably clean in an age when most people weren't. He couldn't even stand to have paint on his fingers. He carried himself like royalty and had elegant manners. Usually he was calm, though he was known to blush when he was insulted (as by his arch-rival, Michelangelo). A welcome addition to parties, he devised clever riddles that made people roar with laughter, and he liked to play pranks that would make people scream — once he unleashed what appeared to be a dragon (actually a large lizard). He rode horses well, sang well, played the lyre well, and, of course, could invent his own musical instruments when necessary.

Leonardo could paint all day without eating, but when he stopped, his favorite meal was minestrone soup. He was a vegetarian, an eccentric choice at the time and one more reason few people understood him. He felt sorry for animals and believed that people who ate them were walking burial places. He was known to buy birds in the market in order to free them, as well as to study their flight.

The thought of flying was one of only two things known to put Leonardo in really high spirits (the other was his design for a submarine). In personal relationships most people seemed to find him melancholy and perhaps a bit cold. In his notebooks the only reference to the woman believed to be his mother is a precise list of her funeral expenses (he made a note of every penny he spent).

Leonardo had no family of his own but informally adopted a peasant boy who lived with him for twenty-six years. The boy was known as Salai (Devil), because he constantly stole, even from Leonardo. The older man pampered him anyway, one year buying him twenty-four pairs of shoes, another time a coat of silver cloth lined with velvet. Between his jobs working for patrons at the various courts of Italy and France, Leonardo traveled; he packed light, taking along his notebooks, his painting of the *Mona Lisa,* and Salai.

While in Florence, Leonardo was accused of heresy against the church, probably for homosexuality, for which the penalty at the time was death. He was acquitted, but after this he became more secretive than ever. Nothing was more important to him than his liberty—two of his earliest inventions had to do with escaping from imprisonment.

Relationships with his patrons were often fraught with misunderstanding and bitterness. Leonardo *was* versatile—in a letter to a potential sponsor he listed thirty-six services he could perform—but notorious for his counterproductive work habits. To get himself out of bed each morning (always a difficulty), he invented a water-operated alarm clock. Such inventions did nothing to end his daydreaming, his dislike of deadlines and schedules, his overambitious ideas, or his tendency to be easily distracted. Sometimes he took money for a work, then never did it, or made promises he knew he couldn't keep. When patrons became too frustrated, they would hire someone else to finish what Leonardo had started.

Leonardo also experienced more than his share of bad luck, and his work gained a reputation as the most vandalized art in history. As a sculptor he was influential and awe-inspiring, but none of his sculpture survived such assaults as being used for target practice by invading armies. Painting techniques he experimented with caused some of his work to disintegrate in his own lifetime. Once, while painting a battle scene on a wall opposite a wall being painted by Michelangelo, he used a new method he had read about. The technique resulted in disaster when all the paints melted together (he hadn't read the instructions all the way through to the part that said "don't try this on walls").

His last boss, the king of France, remained a great admirer through all of these trials, and Leonardo's final three years were his most serene. Then one or both of his hands became paralyzed and his health declined. He died at age sixty-seven. The story that he died in the arms of the king is probably a myth; he was with Francesco da Melzo, a pupil and companion for the last part of his life. Francesco wrote to Leonardo's half-brothers: "It is a hurt to anyone to lose such a man, for nature cannot again produce his like."

In his will Leonardo left everything to Francesco, including his notebooks. He was buried in France, where his gravestone reads: "First painter, engineer, and architect of the King."

RTWORKS

Possibly the world's most famous painting is the *Mona Lisa,* who some think was a real woman named Lisa La Gioconda, the wife of a banker. Her half-smile has mystified whole generations. Was she amused by the comedians Leonardo hired to keep her from getting bored during sittings? Was she missing her front teeth (which is what some dentists believe)? Was she pregnant? Was she really a man? Was she in fact Leonardo himself (some see a resemblance)? And why did Leonardo hold on to the painting all his life?

While Leonardo was painting *The Last Supper* for a group of monks, they kept coming around to ask what was taking him so long (three years). Later the monks carved into the painting to make a doorway. The rest of the work was almost destroyed during the French Revolution (when Napoleon's soldiers threw stones at it) and World War II (when a bomb landed nearby). Recently it has been restored inch by inch, with five hundred years of grime removed.

With the five thousand pages of drawings in his notebooks, Leonardo was the world's first scientific illustrator. He did his technical drawings to improve his painting. He was obsessed with flying machines and also drew the first cars, bicycles, machine guns, tanks, and much more.

*M*ICHELANGELO *B*UONARROTI

BORN IN CAPRESE, ITALY, 1475
DIED IN ROME, ITALY, 1564

*Influential Italian sculptor and painter considered
by some the greatest artist who ever lived, especially famous
for the ceiling of the Sistine Chapel*

"I HAVE KNOWN every shame, suffered every hardship," the man known as the Divine Michelangelo once wrote. During his long, mostly lonely life he made few friends and numerous enemies.

With his strong personality and forceful speech, Michelangelo created an impression of messiness, fierce pride, and gloom. Legendary for doing battle with anyone he disagreed with, he was the first to describe himself as "mad and wicked." He could insult a fellow artist to the point where he would get sued for libel (and lose). The broken nose in his famous profile resulted from a fistfight with a rival sculptor. His rivalry with Leonardo was especially intense, and he taunted the older man in public. He once got even with a critic by painting him into a picture, smothered by a coiled snake. Another time a duke who resented Michelangelo's independent spirit would have had him killed if the pope hadn't intervened.

Michelangelo also had a stormy relationship with his father, whose violent disapproval he had to overcome in order to study art. Yet Michelangelo was always loyal, once writing to him, "All the troubles I have borne, I have borne out of affection for you." During his life he made great

sacrifices to help his father and four brothers (his mother died when he was young).

Michelangelo's love for stone, he often said, came from a stonecutter's wife who had nursed him when he was a baby. His favorite material to work with was expensive marble, and he was at the mercy of wealthy patrons who could afford it. But he could work with anything and once, upon request, created what may have been the world's most magnificent snowman.

Eventually he became wealthy, but he always acted as if he weren't. During his last thirty years he lived in a small, dark house in an alley. It was decorated with cobwebs and his drawing of a man carrying a coffin. He seldom bathed or even took off his dog-skin boots. When he did remove them, sometimes bits of his feet came off, too, as he didn't believe in buying socks. He wore black quilted jackets and broad-brimmed felt hats. He ate crusts of bread while he worked, and at night when he couldn't sleep he put a device on his head that held a candle made of goat grease (which dripped less than wax). It created weird shadows that must have perplexed the neighbors but shed enough light for him to work by.

Michelangelo could be generous in helping younger artists, but he had few real friends until he made time for them late in life. One was a young Roman nobleman, Tommaso de'Cavalieri, and the other was a noblewoman and poet, Vittoria Colonna, whom he greatly respected. He loved to have long conversations with her in her garden, sitting against her ivy-covered wall. Because of his passion for the male form (he used male models even for the women in his art), most people assumed that Michelangelo was homosexual.

Michelangelo remained lean and strong, and even in old age he could split blocks of marble with a single strike of his mallet. He rode horseback in the country every day, whatever the weather. He worked right up to the then-unusual old age of eighty-eight, when he caught a fever after riding in the rain and died a few days later.

ARTWORKS

At age twenty-three Michelangelo finished the sculpture called the *Pietà*. After delivering it himself in a handcart, he overheard an awed spectator say Michelangelo was too young to have created the work. Angry, that night he returned and chiseled his name on it. The *Pietà* is the only work he ever signed.

Michelangelo once fought with Leonardo over a block of marble that had been stored for years in a cathedral work yard. Michelangelo won and worked on his new sculpture for almost three years, the marble chips piling high as he chiseled away. The result was David, the biblical hero, and the work that made Michelangelo world famous.

One of the wonders of the art world was created under what may have been the worst working conditions. While painting the enormous ceiling of the Sistine Chapel at the Vatican in Rome, Michelangelo developed numerous ailments from spending more than four years sixty feet in the air, head bent back, paint splattering his face. Now as many as seven thousand tourists come every day, craning *their* necks to see Michelangelo's ceiling.

PETER BRUEGEL

BORN IN THE NETHERLANDS, 1525?
DIED IN BRUSSELS, BELGIUM, 1569

*Outstanding Flemish painter of the
sixteenth century, most famous for landscapes
and images of peasant life*

DOZENS OF BOOKS have been written about Peter Bruegel, but in his own lifetime he was just one of the 360 painters in the Guild of St. Luke in Antwerp. At least three villages claim to be his birthplace.

The guild, into which he was admitted at about age twenty-five, was a brotherhood in which he spent several years working as an apprentice. He lived with the head of the guild, Peter Coeck van Aelst, Peter's wife, Mayken Verhulst—a well-known painter of miniatures who may have been a major influence on Bruegel—and their baby daughter, Mayken. After he became a master in the guild, Bruegel was free to train his own apprentices, choose his subjects, sign his own name, and accept commissions.

Almost unknown to the public, Bruegel was highly regarded among his few friends as a thoughtful, proper, and unusually silent man. He may have belonged to a discussion group called House of Love, which promoted tolerance during a time of religious persecution; other friends were geographers and printers. Their nickname for him was Peter the Droll, because his pictures made them laugh. Though he was quiet, he was fond of practical jokes, such as pretending to be a ghost and making creepy sounds.

Some of Bruegel's wealthy patrons became personal friends,

relationships rare for the time. One merchant, Hans Franckert, was a daily companion. He and Bruegel, two city men, would disguise themselves in peasant clothes and venture out to nearby villages to attend weddings and fairs as uninvited guests. Bruegel would study the rural people's looks and behavior, making quick sketches he called *naer het leven* (from the life). He and his friend tried to fit in by bringing gifts, eating and dancing, and, if questioned, claiming to be from either the bride's or groom's family.

Bruegel was engaged to a servant girl in Antwerp who had one habit he didn't like—lying. They made an agreement that every time she told a lie, he would make a notch on a stick. If the notches reached the top of the stick, the wedding was off. He used the longest stick he could find, but it wasn't long before he married someone else: Mayken Coeck van Aelst, now twenty, whom he had carried in his arms when she was a baby.

They lived in a three-story brick house on a cobblestone street until Bruegel died of unknown cause a few years later at about age forty-four.

On his deathbed he asked his wife to burn drawings that might get her in trouble with religious authorities who found his tolerant ideas dangerous.

More than two dozen artists descended from Bruegel, starting with his own two sons, who were taught by their grandmother. Peter the Younger became known as Hell Brueghel (the brothers changed the spelling of their name) for painting so many demons, while Jan was known as Velvet Brueghel because of the rich fabrics he portrayed in his art. Jan later commissioned a painting by his friend Peter Paul Rubens to decorate his father's tomb.

But no one thought the facts of Peter Bruegel the Elder's life were worth recording until thirty years after he died, and by then one-third to one-half of all his works had been lost forever.

ARTWORKS

🎨 One reason Bruegel concentrated on peasants, besides his compassion for poor people, was that they were the people most affected by seasonal changes. His love of the seasons led to a series of works known as *Seasons*. Completed for one of his wealthy patrons (to decorate a room in his new mansion), it includes *Hunters in the Snow*, considered one of the greatest landscape paintings in history. The patron later fell on hard times and had to turn the series over to the city of Antwerp.

🎨 In Bruegel's time works of art were meant to be studied, like a book. For example, at least eighty real pastimes of the era have been identified in his *Children's Games*, which shows hundreds of village children playing leapfrog, hide-and-seek, marbles, and many other games.

🎨 *The Artist and the Connoisseur* may be Bruegel's only self-portrait; it shows an uncomfortable artist confronting a smug patron who has financial power over him. Many art historians believe the drawing reveals a case of advanced arthritis in Bruegel's gnarled hands.

SOFONISBA ANGUISSOLA

BORN IN CREMONA, ITALY, 1532
DIED IN PALERMO, ITALY, 1625

Influential Italian Renaissance painter,
world renowned for introducing
new techniques in portraits

SOFONISBA ANGUISSOLA HAD a lot of things working against her. In her day women, considered inferior versions of men, were thought to have little intelligence and no talent. Having lost some of the rights they had gained during the Middle Ages, most women were not even taught to read. They had no say in their own futures; in their teens they either married or entered a convent. Even fashions, such as whalebone corsets that restricted breathing and movement, worked against women. Anguissola had no role models to guide her in what she wanted to do—paint—and she was further handicapped by a lifelong inflammation of the eyelids, possibly from allergies.

Anguissola did, however, have parents who were known as enlightened. Her merchant father and his wife made sure their six daughters got the same private tutoring as their one son. The public considered the sisters intellectual marvels, almost like circus freaks, and travelers would go out of their way to visit the family. Anguissola's greatest champion was her father, who always talked her up around town to the clergy and nobility. She was even allowed to journey an arduous three weeks on unpaved roads to Rome to study with Michelangelo, who was most encouraging.

As her reputation spread for painting likenesses that truly seemed alive, Anguissola continued to live with her family, except when she traveled to do commissioned portraits. Her arrival probably stirred much gossip. She would wear dresses of brocade and silk, and always had her boxes of paint, her canvases, and a chaperon. She prepared her own painting materials (from such ingredients as dried rabbit skins, copper, lead, and linseed or walnut oil) and wore smocks to protect her elegant gowns. Sometimes she was paid with money, sometimes with jewels and expensive fabrics. Those who met her said she had a quick spirit and was kind.

Then she was invited to become court painter to King Philip II of Spain, the most powerful ruler in Europe. It was a great honor, and she remained at court for twenty years. When the queen, Isabel, died in childbirth, she left Anguissola some fine brocade for a bedcover, as a hint to get married. At the relatively old age of thirty-eight, Anguissola married a man the king selected (with her preferences in mind): Don Fabrizio de Moncada, a Sicilian nobleman. She may have had a child, but historical records are unclear.

When her husband died, probably from the plague, Anguissola traveled back to Italy to visit her family. On the way she was swept off her feet by the ship's captain, a much younger man named Orazio Lomellino, and by the trip's end had agreed to marry him. The marriage was happy—and while her husband was at sea, Anguissola had plenty of free time for painting.

Except for her eye condition, Anguissola must have been unusually strong. At a time when the average life span for women was thirty years, she lived to age ninety-three. Eventually she was forced to get a document called a *fides vitae*, literally a certificate to prove she was still alive, in order to continue cashing the king's pension.

In her old age she was much sought out as an adviser to younger women, and her reputation encouraged generations after her to consider a career in the arts.

ARTWORKS

In *The Chess Game,* which features her sisters Lucia, Minerva, and Europa enjoying a game of chess, Anguissola introduced a new element into portraits: laughter. Smiles were rare in portraits then, but Anguissola was always experimenting with a warm and lively style. Even in court, where portraits had to be serious, she worked in traces of grins and quirky personalities. Not for another one hundred years did other portrait painters show people in happy moods.

Also unique for incorporating still lifes into her portraits, Anguissola in *Self-Portrait at the Clavichord* made yet another innovation: portraying a person in action. In a move away from the formal, static style of the day, she liked to highlight her subjects' hobbies. Anguissola painted more self-portraits than almost any artist of her time, in part because she was considered so amazing that people wanted paintings done both by her and of her.

REMBRANDT VAN RIJN

BORN IN LEIDEN, HOLLAND, 1606
DIED IN AMSTERDAM, HOLLAND, 1669

The greatest master of the Dutch school of art,
painter of historical scenes and expressive
portraits of himself and others

REMBRANDT VAN RIJN experienced one of history's most rapid rises to the top. At age thirteen he left school to study art; at seventeen he started his own studio; and by his mid-twenties he was the leading portrait painter to the richest families in the richest city in Europe, Amsterdam.

For the next twenty years it seemed that everything Rembrandt touched turned to gold. With people begging him to paint them, he worked nonstop and could turn out a portrait every two weeks. The sons of the rich flocked to him as pupils, and he took on up to fifty at a time. His students imitated him as much as possible and even dressed like him. Although there were complaints that Rembrandt sometimes signed their paintings and sold them as his own—and some resentment of his constant experimentation (why did his heroes and heroines, for instance, look so much like his ordinary neighbors?)—he laughed between his trips to the bank.

Rembrandt married Saskia, the wealthy cousin of the man who sold his paintings, and together they bought one of the biggest houses in town. They furnished it luxuriously with green velvet chairs in the latest style, built-in beds with piles of down pillows, and a legendary art collection. Art dealers raised their prices when they saw Rembrandt coming—he enjoyed outbidding everyone else, just for the fun of it. He also collected expensive clothes, jewelry for Saskia, and props to use in his paintings: seashells, weapons, and musical instruments. The house had enough bedrooms for many children, but over the years, as their infants failed to survive, he turned the rooms into storage space for his collections.

Rembrandt drew himself wearing furs and gold chains and other exotic accessories, but in real life he usually wore old clothes stained with paint. A quiet homebody, he made meals out of herring, bread, and cheese.

Saskia died young and left their one surviving infant son, Titus. Devastated and almost sick with loneliness, Rembrandt fell into two relationships apparently at the same time—with Titus's nanny, Geertje, and with the family's maid, Hendrickje. The terms of Saskia's will required that he didn't remarry, but Geertje took him to court, saying that he had promised to marry her. Rembrandt was ordered to support her, but with her brother's help he had her committed to an asylum instead. The scandal deepened when he and Hendrickje—who had a daughter, Cornelia, with him—never married. Gossiping friends avoided him, and the local church summoned her four times for rebuke.

Rembrandt's work gradually fell out of fashion, and his stubbornness didn't help his reputation. Once when he refused to remove a monkey from the portrait of a family that had no monkey, they refused to buy the painting.

Always careless with his money, Rembrandt eventually went bankrupt. After he was forced to sell everything he owned at a fraction of its worth, he spent his last thirteen years in dignified poverty, pretending not to be at home when creditors called.

Hendrickje and Titus both died, and Rembrandt lived on with Cornelia, his eyesight failing. When he died at age sixty-three, possibly of the plague, there was no public notice and he was buried in an unmarked grave.

ARTWORKS

 *Anatomy Lesson of Dr. Tulp*, a portrait of surgeons dissecting a body (of a criminal known as the Kid), was Rembrandt's first important commission. This was a time when people paid to see dissections at anatomy theaters, which were unheated to prevent the corpse from decaying too fast.

The Night Watch, probably the most famous Dutch Painting of all time, doesn't show a night scene—and no one is keeping watch. The title was added 150 years after the painting was completed, when it had darkened with age. All the models paid Rembrandt to be included in the painting; the people in the front of the picture contributed more money than the ones in the back.

Although it was thought for years to be one of Rembrandt's greatest works, *Man with a Golden Helmet* is now believed to be by one of his students. Since 1968 a team of scholars known as the Rembrandt Research Project has been studying his work; so far they have reduced the number of genuine Rembrandt paintings from 700 to 350—much to the dismay of many museums.

OLD MAN MAD ABOUT DRAWING

Katsushika Hokusai

BORN IN 1760 AND DIED IN 1849
IN EDO, JAPAN

Japanese painter and printmaker,
known for his enormous influence on both
Eastern and Western art

THE MAN HISTORY knows as Katsushika Hokusai was born in the Year of the Dragon in the bustling city now known as Tokyo.

After working for eight stormy years in the studio of a popular artist who resented the boy's greater skill, Hokusai was finally thrown out. At first he earned his daily bowl of rice as a street peddler, selling red peppers and ducking if he saw his old teacher coming. Soon he was illustrating comic books, then turning out banners, made-to-order greeting cards for the rich, artwork for novels full of murders and ghosts, and drawings of scenes throughout his beloved Edo.

Changing one's name was a Japanese custom, but Hokusai carried it to an extreme—he changed his more than thirty times. No one knows why. Perhaps he craved variety, or was self centered (thinking that every change in his art style required a new identity), or merely liked being eccentric. One name he kept longer than most was Hokusai, meaning "Star of the Northern Constellation," in honor of a Buddhist god he especially revered.

He did like variety in dwellings. Notorious for never cleaning his studio, he took the easy way out whenever the place became too disgustingly dirty: he moved. Hokusai moved a total of ninety-three times—putting a burden on his family and creating a new set of neighbors for himself at least once a year. He married twice and had seven children, most of whom died in their twenties.

A born showman, Hokusai attracted attention by staging public performances of his art. Spectators marveled when he drew birds in flight—on a grain of rice; crowds cheered when he sprawled on a huge sheet of paper to paint with a brush the size of a broom. Sometimes he painted while hanging upside down, or with the brush held in his mouth or between his toes.

Wealth didn't impress him. He was known to keep important clients waiting while he meticulously picked all the fleas off his kimono. He lived simply, usually in poor neighborhoods. Hokusai drank tea and ate little, mostly rice cakes; he enjoyed a bowl of noodle soup before he went to bed. In the style of the times, he slept on a straw mat brought out from the closet every night. Money held no interest for him. When he had to pay bills, he would hand over one of the unopened envelopes of payments he had received for his art—sometimes the money in the envelope matched the amount of the bill, sometimes it didn't.

Hokusai once went bankrupt and, to escape arrest by creditors,

changed his name yet again and went into hiding outside of town for a year. Though he nearly died of starvation, running out of paper and paints was his worst nightmare. After dark he would walk fifteen miles into Edo for supplies, trying to return before anyone he owed money to recognized him.

The older Hokusai got, the harder he worked. Sitting on his heels, hour after hour, he completed over thirty thousand pieces of art—an average of one a day during the course of his life. He hoped for immortality but made it to age eighty-nine. The inscription on his gravestone shows his final name, Gwakio Rojin, meaning "Old Man Mad about Drawing."

ARTWORKS

Hokusai's most famous images come from a series of prints called *Thirty-Six Views of Mount Fuji*, which reveal this sacred symbol of Japan from various angles. *The Great Wave*, the "view" most often reproduced, shows Fuji framed in the curve of a wave about to engulf three fishing boats.

Manga (or *Random Sketches*) was a fifteen-volume encyclopedia of Hokusai's drawings of Japanese life—dragons, pagodas, wrestlers and acrobats, whole pages of "Thin People" or "Fat Men." In 1856 a friend of French artist Edgar Degas found Hokusai prints such as these being used as packing material in a crate of porcelain from Japan. The prints became all the rage among most artists of the time, and Hokusai became the most important figure in introducing Eastern art to the Western world. Today each of those prints would be worth as much as fifty thousand dollars.

MARY CASSATT

BORN IN ALLEGHENY CITY, PENNSYLVANIA, 1845
DIED IN MENSIL-THÉRIBUS, FRANCE, 1926

*Renowned American painter whose favorite subjects
were motherhood and childhood*

MARY CASSATT VALUED her independence all her life. Anxious to escape prim and proper Philadelphia society, she moved to Paris, the European capital of art, just as soon as she could. As a painter she was a woman in a man's world, and because of her love of all things French, she became an American in France.

When Cassatt announced her intention to be an artist, her father is supposed to have said, "I would almost rather see you dead." Her family's idea of a good work of art was one with horses in it, and they weren't especially interested in what Marne (Cassatt's family nickname) did. But they didn't stand in her way and indeed were almost always around, in part to act as chaperons (which society required for unmarried women).

Cassatt's reaction to meeting French artist Edgar Degas was to write later, "I began to live." He called her "a supplier of good days" (meaning for himself); she called him "my best, my only, friend." People assumed that there was a romance between Cassatt and Degas, but the truth will never be known. She burned all of his letters before she died, and none of hers to him have ever come to light.

"Too much pudding," Cassatt said about the increasing praise for her work, as if fame was too sweet for her. But she did relish ordering fancy clothes from the best shops—she bought large, elaborate hats and simple but elegant dresses, often in gray. Eventually, with her earnings, she purchased a red brick home in the country, called Chateau de Beaufresne (House of the Beautiful Ash Tree). There she would entertain writers, diplomats, and painters until 2:00 A.M. and be at work the next morning, wearing her white crepe smock. She ate oysters for lunch; for dessert she liked chocolate-caramel sweets, or perhaps a Philadelphia treat known as white mountain cake.

The neighbors' view of Cassatt was often that of a woman leaning down from a tall horse. Horses were her passion, means of escape, and source of exercise. Their danger and speed appealed to her, and they enabled her to be close to her father, with whom she frequently rode. At age forty-three she was seriously injured when a snake bit her horse and the animal threw her. This didn't stop her from riding, but she began dividing her interest between horses and Belgian griffons, a breed of dog that always looks as if it might nip. Cassatt could seem a little nippish herself—if she disagreed with her dinner guests, she would bang her fist on the table.

Although she was famous for her drawings of children, Cassatt had no desire to be a wife or mother. Her only known romantic relationship came late in her life, with a banker who shopped at Tiffany's for jeweled collars and feeding bowls for her Pekingese (named Batty). She hated being called a woman artist instead of just an artist, and she supported the right of women to vote. She gave generous financial help to women factory workers, and she looked forward to a future in which women would take part in government.

Late in life Cassatt went blind and so had to stop painting. She died at age eighty-one, alone except for her faithful housekeeper, Mathilde, and three other servants. Beaufresne was eventually turned into a home for abandoned children.

RTWORKS

Cassatt once painted a portrait of a family friend who rejected the work because of the nose — the friend thought it looked a bit like a pig's snout. Upset, Cassatt stuck the painting in a storeroom for more than twenty years and didn't pick up a brush for months. Known as *Lady at the Tea-Table*, it now hangs in a museum.

A *Goodnight Hug*, Cassatt's first mother-and-child work, was painted three years after she met Degas. He had advised her that the maternal theme, which had never been done except in a religious way, would set her apart and compensate for the lack of recognition she would face as a woman painter.

The first of many pictures of her favorite niece was *Ellen Mary Cassatt in a White Coat*, for which the infant posed without complaint. Most children found posing for Cassatt an agreeable experience, as she supplied chocolates, books, and toys. Some, however, were made nervous by her crowd of nipping griffons.

Vincent van Gogh

BORN IN GROOT-ZUNDERT, HOLLAND, 1853
DIED IN AUVERS-SUR-OISE, FRANCE, 1890

*Dutch painter whose works and life are possibly
better known than any other artist's*

THIS IS WHAT most people remember about Vincent van Gogh: One night he and the French artist Paul Gauguin had a bitter fight in a café. According to Gauguin, Van Gogh chased him down an alley, brandishing a razor. When Gauguin turned and stared him down, Van Gogh went home and used the razor to slice off the lobe of his left ear. Wrapping the earlobe in a handkerchief, he took it to Rachel, a prostitute he had befriended, and said, "Guard this object carefully." She fainted, and he went home to his bed and almost bled to death. But two weeks later he had recovered, apologized to Rachel, and was back in his most productive period as an artist.

The other thing many people know about Van Gogh is that his art never achieved recognition during his life. He sold only one painting out of the hundreds of works he created. His younger brother Theo was often his only source of encouragement; he was ignored or rejected by nearly everyone else.

But after age twenty-eight, once he had settled on painting as the way he was meant to serve humanity, Van Gogh never stopped. He had tried being an art dealer, a bookstore clerk, a teacher, a lay preacher, and a social worker among poor miners. As an artist he was almost entirely self-taught, was always defying the rules, and always believed in himself despite bouts of mental illness that sometimes made him depressed and suicidal. He drew on cafe menus, books, and scraps of paper; he frequently walked into the countryside to paint, looking like a porcupine with his easels and brushes poking out all over. The privacy in the country was worth enduring the strong winds, irritating mosquitoes, and crows that pestered him while he worked.

Nearly everything Van Gogh did differed from how others behaved, and people usually reacted to him with either laughter or fear. Villagers sometimes played practical jokes on "the little painter fellow"; nervous priests warned parishioners not to pose for him; children taunted Van Gogh in the streets, throwing cabbage stalks and chanting, "He's mad! He's mad!"

Most people would have agreed with Van Gogh's description of himself as a "shaggy dog." He wore scruffy clothes: usually a blue artist's smock, a furry overcoat, and a battered straw hat. Once he made a suit for himself out of lilac-colored cloth with yellow spots. At his best Van Gogh was vague and moody, with a tendency to laugh at inappropriate moments. At his worst he was argumentative and stubborn, managing to alienate almost everyone no matter how good-hearted his intentions. Even Theo, who believed his brother was a genius, thought he could be his own worst enemy.

Van Gogh's attempts to marry never worked out. One landlady's daughter, Eugenie, did not return his affection, nor did his cousin Kee, whose rejection of his proposal was definite and haunting: "No—at no time—never." He tried unsuccessfully to form a stable family with a pregnant prostitute, Sien, and her daughter. The only woman to fall in love with *him* was Margot Begemann, a neighbor ten years older than he was. Out of sympathy for her, Van Gogh didn't discourage her infatuation. When their families intervened, she tried to commit suicide and the scandal rocked the village.

Always desperately poor (he earned almost no money during his lifetime), Van Gogh was supported by Theo, who became a successful art dealer.

Van Gogh imposed a condition of near starvation on himself and would go for days without food so he could afford to buy art supplies. Sometimes he gave clothes and food away to those even poorer than himself. When he did eat, his meals consisted of bread and cheese; he rejected meat, sugar, and butter as luxuries, though he did allow himself cheap tobacco for the pipe he always smoked. As a cook he was undistinguished—people who tasted his soup suspected it was made with paint because it tasted so terrible.

Van Gogh had insomnia, rotten teeth (eventually he had ten pulled), and a constant upset stomach from drinking many cups of strong black coffee. He lived as a vagabond, but among his few possessions were some four hundred Japanese prints, which he pinned up on the walls wherever he was staying. His own works that he left behind were not valued by anyone who found them; they ended up lost, burned for fuel, or used to repair chicken coops or outhouses.

The closest Van Gogh ever came to having a place of his own was a four-room rented house in Aries, in the south of France. For two years he lived in what was known around town as the Yellow House — a period of intense creative output unmatched in the history of Western art. Besides completing almost a painting a day, he dreamed of starting a commune of contemporary artists, with a skeptical Gauguin and himself as its founders.

Already considered a misfit by the close-knit community that found his melancholy ways offensive, Van Gogh was even less popular after the ear episode. When the incident was reported in the local newspaper, unsympathetic neighbors decided Van Gogh was not merely moody but dangerous. They organized a petition to have him removed from town. By then Gauguin had fled and Van Gogh knew that his commune plans were failing. He admitted himself to an asylum fifteen miles away — and remained productive even there, where he was allowed to have a studio.

Over the years many doctors have speculated about the mysterious nature of Van Gogh's breakdowns, which came and went, interfering with his life and art. Besides various ear disorders, the diagnoses have included epilepsy, schizophrenia, manic-depressive disorder, syphilis, a chemical imbalance due to extreme sensitivity to light, and poisoning from occasionally swallowing his own paints. Any of these may have been made worse by malnutrition, combined with overwork and too much drink — his favorite was absinthe, a deadly, emerald green alcohol nicknamed the Green Fairy, which could cause hallucinations.

He was in and out of asylums until, at age thirty-seven, he borrowed a revolver, went out into the fields, and shot himself in the stomach. Refusing medical help, he died two days later in Theo's arms. In his pocket was the last of the hundreds of letter he had written to his brother: "Well, my own work, I am risking my life for it and half my reason is gone."

His suicide devastated Theo, who died six months later, at age thirty-three, from the effects of sorrow and stress. Johanna, Theo's widow, devoted the rest of her life to establishing Van Gogh's reputation, and within thirty years of his death he was acknowledged as one of the giants of modern art.

RTWORKS

Van Gogh considered *The Potato Eaters* his first masterpiece. "It speaks of manual labor and how they have honestly earned their food," he wrote of the De Groots, the members of the peasant family who were his models. Unusually patient, they let him draw them over a whole winter—longer than he worked on any other painting. As he was often too poor to hire models, Van Gogh painted twenty-two portraits of himself, including *Self-Portrait with Severed Ear.*

Van Gogh found one of his favorite subjects while exploring his beloved countryside: sunflowers. To him they symbolized gratitude—to his brother for support, to Gauguin for friendship, to the sun for light and warmth. He wanted to sell his series of sunflower paintings for a little badly needed money (about eighty dollars then) but had no luck. In 1987 the piece known as *Sunflowers* sold for nearly forty million dollars—almost three million dollars per flower.

Starry Night, considered by many to be Van Gogh's best work, was painted while he was confined to an asylum room, never bored with what he could see out his window. *Irises,* which he painted in an asylum garden, sold in 1988 for forty-nine million dollars—the buyer called it "the most important painting in the world."

Käthe Kollwitz

*German creator of sculpture, drawings, woodcuts,
and posters that expressed her desire
for social justice*

AS A TEEN Käthe Schmidt met and became engaged to Karl Kollwitz; she married him when she was twenty-four. Her engagement ring created an uproar at the girls' art school she attended—students considered marriage an abandonment of art. After much thought she hoped that she would have more freedom as a married woman than as a single one still under the control of her father. But she made it clear to Karl that she valued herself as an artist more than as a wife. Perhaps for this reason the first few of their forty-nine years together were stormy, though mostly the couple was happy.

They spent all forty-nine years in the same Berlin building, where they lived on the third floor above a busy intersection of cobblestone streets. On the second floor Kollwitz's studio—crammed with old bathtubs and garbage cans full of clay or water as well as sculptures-in-progress—was next to Karl's free medical clinic for poor people. Quiet was hard for Kollwitz to come by, especially when the clinic was full of mothers with ailing babies, and later when she was raising two sons of her own. Sometimes she went next door and drew the women as they waited to see her husband, or they would wander in to talk to her and she would help ease their grief and

worry. As soon as they could afford to do so, the Kollwitzes hired Lina, a live-in housekeeper.

Kollwitz startled neighbors by not wearing a hat over her unfashionable hair; sometimes she did not bother to remove the paint-splattered smock she wore over her simple tailored dresses. Ambitious and serious, she talked plainly, without much humor or openness about personal matters. She was shy with most strangers. When she was occasionally asked to teach art, she would become sweaty with nervousness.

Kollwitz played in all her sons' games, designing kites for them, installing acrobatic bars in the hallway, singing folk songs. With them she enjoyed her favorite sport: mountain climbing in the Austrian Alps. When the younger son, Peter, was killed at age eighteen in World War I, Kollwitz never really recovered from the loss.

She was passionately antiwar, deeply concerned with the poor and helpless, and sincere about devoting her art to what she called "the many quiet and loud tragedies of city life." She created posters to support the feminist movement, homosexual rights efforts, the right to abortion, and the rights of children, who were often forced to work as family breadwinners.

When she and Karl publicly opposed the Nazis, they were not surprised to start getting visits from the Gestapo (the secret police). Her art was banned, his clinic was closed, and they were threatened with death or imprisonment in a concentration camp. The Kollwitzes never were taken away, possibly because neighbors came to their defense. But they began carrying vials of poison, with the intention of swallowing the poison if they ever fell into the hands of the Nazis.

Bombing raids on Berlin were severe during World War II, and Kollwitz moved outside the city just in time before her building was destroyed. She died five years after Karl, of heart failure, at age seventy-eight. *The Group*, her last sculpture, now stands in a small park in Berlin called Käthe Kollwitz Square, on Käthe Kollwitz Street.

ARTWORKS

Kollwitz used herself as a model probably more than any other woman artist — she did eighty-four self-portraits in all. The first, called *Self-Portrait, Laughing*, done when she was seventeen, is the only smiling image of herself; others are serious, even sad. She used herself and seven-year-old Peter as models for *Mother with Dead Child*. Drawing with one hand while holding the boy with the other proved such a strain that it made her groan. Peter murmured reassuringly, "Don't worry, Mother, it will be beautiful," and in fact the finished drawing was so painfully real that friends couldn't bear to look at it.

Kollwitz's largest works were a granite memorial for Peter — sculptures of two grieving parents, called *The Mother* and *The Father*, placed at the entrance to the cemetery where Peter is buried. The unveiling of the companion works established her as a prominent sculptor, just as years before *Revolt of the Weavers* (a series of prints about peasants who rebel against their wretched living conditions) had made her an overnight success as a printmaker.

Henri Matisse

BORN IN LE CATEAU-CAMBRÉSIS, FRANCE, 1869
DIED IN NICE, FRANCE, 1954

*French painter and sculptor considered one of
the foremost modern artists, especially
famous for paper cutouts*

WHEN HENRI MATISSE quit law school and left for Paris to study art, his father shook his fist at the train and said, "You'll die of hunger!"

Matisse did live on a diet of rice when he had to, resisting the temptation to eat the fruit he bought for his still lifes. At his poorest he considered staging an accident to destroy paintings so he could collect the insurance money. Critics dubbed him King of the Wild Beasts; Matisse responded by wearing a sheepskin coat with the fleecy side out to make himself even beastier. Graffiti appeared on bathroom walls: "Matisse causes insanity!"

Through it all Matisse's ego stayed intact. Once he boasted that his paintings lit up a room (a friend replied that he himself preferred a lamp). Some people found Matisse's self-absorption intensely boring, but his friends admired him for being completely without pretense.

His wife, Amelie, supported him by opening a hat shop. She also raised Marguerite (his daughter with a previous girlfriend) and their sons, Jean (who became a sculptor) and Pierre (who became a prominent art dealer). Totally devoted to Matisse, Amelie never complained, not even about his chronic insomnia, when he would wake her in the middle of the

night to read out loud to him or go for long walks with him—sometimes to the next town.

To limber up his fingers Matisse began each day by playing the violin for two hours. In a hotel he'd play in remote bathrooms so as not to bother his neighbors, then get to work. Posing for Matisse could be torture. He would talk to himself, curse, and weep. Very nearsighted, he sat close to his models (often supplied by movie extra agencies), sometimes with his knee pressed against the other person. If he was concentrating and a model asked something as simple as the time of day, he would be devastated. To relieve his tension he took up the sport of rowing, and he did it well enough to win medals for his skill.

Ultimately Matisse became the highest paid living artist of his time. He began dressing in expensive suits and serving champagne, although it took him a while to get the hang of opening the bottles. He moved to a country house outside Paris and bought horses. When he went riding with Pablo Picasso—his lifelong friend and rival—he would deliberately tire Picasso out by riding a little too fast. In his car he drove slowly and took up the whole road, savoring "a sense of the trees." The tropical birds he kept flew free around the rooms of his house.

In middle age Matisse moved to the French Riviera, where he liked the light. He stayed there the rest of his life, living in hotels where his wife and children came to visit. His companion was Lydia, who modeled for him and assisted him in everything, even as nurse to Amelie, who was often ill. When they thought no one was around, Matisse and Lydia played hide-and-seek. Eventually Amelie could no longer tolerate Matisse's attention toward Lydia, and they were legally separated.

During World War II, when France was occupied by Germany, Matisse was so nervous that he went to movies every night to distract himself. But he didn't leave France, as many other artists did, and later was acclaimed as a hero. He had a heart attack and died in his daughter Marguerite's arms at age eighty-four.

ARTWORKS

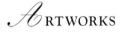

One of Matisse's many portraits of Amelie was *The Woman with the Hat,* which critics found scandalously unrealistic and insulting to women. An American named Leo called it "the nastiest smear of paint I had ever seen," but he and his sister—writer Gertrude Stein—bought the painting anyway.

One of Matisse's most famous paintings, *Dance II,* portrays a peasant dance he remembered from his childhood village, the tune of which he whistled as he painted. He worried that its vibrant colors would frighten viewers, and in fact the work caused such a furor when it was first exhibited that he left the country for two months, fleeing to Spain, where he took three hot baths a day to calm his nerves.

When he was too frail and upset by the war to paint, Matisse became preoccupied with paper cutouts, such as *Icarus,* a work in his book *Jazz.* At first he used cutouts as a way to aid his work on paintings, but later he thought of them as art in themselves. He felt that it had taken all of his life to achieve their simplicity, and he covered his walls with huge cutouts in colors so bright that he had to wear sunglasses to look at them.

$\mathscr{P}$ABLO $\mathscr{P}$ICASSO

BORN IN MÁLAGA, SPAIN, 1881
DIED IN MOUGINS, FRANCE, 1973

Spanish painter, sculptor, graphic artist, and ceramicist—
considered the foremost figure
of twentieth-century art

PABLO PICASSO GREW up indulged by the five women in his household. He hated authority and was not a good student—possibly because of dyslexia, he had trouble learning to read and write. Instead of doing his schoolwork, he would bring a pigeon to class and spend his time drawing it.

He had his first exhibit at age thirteen, when he showed his paintings in the back room of an umbrella store. Later he hung out at the Café Four Cats and had an exhibit there, too, but the only works that sold were to people whose portraits he had done. He left for Paris at age eighteen, wearing his black corduroy suit. Just before his departure, he wrote on his most recent self-portrait: "I the king. I the king. I the king."

In Paris, though, he lived less than royally. His home was a garret; he worked by the light of a single candle he stuck into a bottle. Occasionally he could not even afford the candle. He used books for pillows, sometimes burned drawings to keep warm, kept a white mouse as a pet, and ate fried potatoes, beans, and omelettes. When his place was robbed, thieves stole everything but his art.

Whenever he had enough money he went to the bullfights, which he had loved as a child, fascinated by the bullfighters' lack of fear. One of his nicknames for himself was Eye of the Bull, and he liked to play his friends against each other, using one as a red flag and the other as a bull. Some thought Picasso was even built like a bullfighter, strong and powerful.

He did seem massive but was only five feet two inches tall. Although he never exercised, he was always fit and had unusual stamina. He could stand in front of a canvas for seven or eight hours at a stretch. "Work is the most important" was his favorite motto, and he was hugely productive.

A master of publicity, Picasso decided early on that the amount of money a painting sold for was directly related to the legend surrounding the artist: "It's not what an artist does that counts, but what he is." And so, with his penetrating stare and a lit cigarette constantly between his lips, he radiated self-confidence and cultivated a fiery image. He liked to be in absolute command of every situation. Although usually he got the adulation he craved, sometimes it was too much; once when he was surrounded by a cheering crowd, he took out the gun he carried whenever he left his studio and fired it into the air. Within seconds the area around him was deserted.

Picasso knew everyone. He hid in air-raid shelters with the writer Gertrude Stein—a longtime friend—during World War I and gave her advice when her poodle died. He often walked the composer Erik Satie home, doffing his hat and saying, "Good night, Mr. Satie," and he drew a portrait of composer Igor Stravinsky that military authorities were sure was a secret map. Writer Ernest Hemingway came to visit immediately after World War II and brought him a box of hand grenades. Yet he was notorious for cruelty to friends, other artists, bystanders; it was said that living with him meant wearing armor twenty-four hours a day.

Some of Picasso's romantic relationships were with famous women (the ballerina Olga Koklova, the painter and photographer Dora Maar, the painter Françoise Gilot), and some were not. He would walk up to a woman and say, "I'm Picasso! You and I are going to do great things together." He was not good at making decisions and was sometimes involved with two or three women at the same time, preferring to let the women fight it out. Neighbors didn't always approve of his lifestyle and at least once threw stones at his windows in protest. Jacqueline, his second and last wife, was the only person he could stand to have around when he painted.

Picasso went to great lengths to entertain his four small children—dressing up in women's underwear, drawing on tablecloths, performing magic tricks with paper towels, preparing birthday dinners made up entirely of different kinds of chocolate desserts. As his children grew older, however, he lost some of his interest in them.

His favorite clothes were striped sailors' jerseys, baggy trousers, Turkish slippers, and berets (especially after he started losing his hair). He kept his wallet in the inside pocket of his coat, fastened with a safety pin for extra security; friends were amused at the trouble he had to go to every time

he wanted to pay for something. He had certain suspicions—he believed, for example, that if his hair clippings fell into the wrong hands, they could be used against him. He didn't like the telephone and didn't get one until one son almost died when the family couldn't call for medical help. He threw nothing away, not even empty cigarette packs and the paper and ribbons from packages. He always locked his studio, and absolutely no one was allowed to dust it.

He kept to a diet of fish, vegetables, rice pudding, grapes, raspberries crushed in milk, large pieces of fresh ginger, carrot and pea soup, and mineral water. His midafternoon snack was lime-blossom tea and toast.

Restless, he moved often. He bought one of his three mansions in the south of France for the price commanded by one of his still lifes, which tickled him. In one chateau he covered the walls of the luxurious bathroom—where his wife would give him his bath—with wild jungle beasts. In his last villa, Notre-Dame-de-Vie, he was protected by electronic gates and guard dogs. There was hardly any tamable animal he didn't shelter at some point, including a monkey, Esmeralda the goat, reptiles, and numerous Afghan hounds. As soon as he could afford it he hired a chauffeur: "Driving a car is very bad for a painter's wrists!"

Picasso might have liked this book, or at least this chapter. After 1945 about six books on Picasso were published each year, and he enjoyed reading them. Knowing that anything he said would eventually show up in in the papers, he subscribed to a service that clipped articles for him. At the public premiere of a documentary about him, he amused the audience by calling out for a second showing—and then a third.

Gradually he cut himself off from almost everyone except his fans; he even refused to meet his grandchildren. At his eightieth birthday party— for which four thousand invitations were sent—he arrived escorted by police. He remained vital and prolific and in his ninetieth year did two hundred paintings. He was still working the day he died, two years later, of heart failure. His last words were to his doctor: "You are wrong not to be married. It's useful."

He died without a will, and his estate, valued at hundreds of millions of dollars, was eventually divided between Jacqueline, three children, and two grandchildren.

ARTWORKS

🎨 Picasso's early days of Paris poverty are known as the Blue Period because everything he painted—self-portraits, beggars, harlequins, and musicians such as *The Old Guitarist*—came out sad and blue.

🎨 Then followed the Pink Period, when Picasso began his first real romantic relationship (with a neighbor) and grew happier. Its first picture is considered to be *The Young Girl with a Basket of Flowers*, bought by Gertrude Stein. Paris papers called another Pink Period work, *Family of Saltimbanques*, "grotesque and infamous," but the spectacular price paid for the painting of six circus performers changed Picasso's life.

🎨 *Guernica* is Picasso's response to the German bombing of a Spanish town by that name, in which sixteen hundred civilians died. During the German occupation of Paris during World War II, Picasso kept a large photo of *Guernica* on the wall of his studio. A Nazi officer once saw it and said, "So it was you who did that," to which Picasso replied, "No, you did it."

🎨 The model for Picasso's famous peace dove, created for a Peace Congress held after World War II, was one of Matisse's birds. Posters of it were all over Paris when Picasso's daughter was born; he named her Paloma (Spanish for dove).

CLOWNING AROUND

*M*ARC *C*HAGALL

BORN IN PESTKOVATIK, RUSSIA, 1887
DIED IN ST. PAUL DE VENCE, FRANCE, 1985

*Russian painter renowned for paintings of
Russian-Jewish folklore, theater sets,
stained-glass windows, and murals*

MARC CHAGALL BEGAN to draw while he was perched on the stove, the only place he was not in the way, handing down drawings to his six sisters. Considered the talented darling of his devoutly Hasidic Jewish family, he was an unusually beautiful child, and in his teens began rouging his cheeks and lips to make them even redder.

As a teenager he left Russia to study art in Paris. There he worked each night until dawn, often in the nude, at La Ruche, a beehive-like building with tiny studios. If a painting turned into a mess, he'd simply hurl it out the window and it would be taken away with the garbage. Their neighbors in the slaughterhouse district (where the smell of blood was ever present) thought the artists were useless do-nothings and that Chagall was one of the strangest.

Early critics called his work everything from thoughtless to pornographic, but Chagall was soon unable to keep up with his commissions. He could be businesslike, even selling the doodles he had made on cafe napkins. Jealous rivals called him *too* businesslike (stingy) and a great teller of stories about himself. He didn't exchange pictures with other artists—"I like my own too much"—and if he didn't like someone else's art, he called it peepee.

Chagall's first wife was the elegant Bella Rosenfeld, whose face dominated his work. "Unfortunately, she's always right," he said of Bella and her artistic influence. Besides posing as his model, she kept him supplied with sweet cakes and grilled fish and handled all his practical affairs. He found the crying of their baby daughter Ida intolerable, but as Ida grew older he took her to the circus every week.

Chagall lived through so much tumult—wars, revolutions, persecution—that sometimes people were surprised to learn he was still alive. "My canvases vibrate with sobs," he claimed. For the most part, though, he ignored historical events, living in a nonpolitical bubble with Bella. During the Nazi occupation of France, when dozens of Jewish artists were being killed, Chagall seemed unaware, as though he believed that his fame would keep him safe. By the time he realized that he was in danger, it was almost too late. He and Bella were arrested during a Nazi raid—then released as a result of American intervention.

The Chagalls fled to the United States until it was safe to return. Chagall enjoyed strolling through Jewish neighborhoods on the Lower East Side of New York City, eating strudel, and bargaining with merchants in their stalls. But when Bella died suddenly of a virus, Chagall's hair immediately went silver and friends worried that he would die of grief.

Instead he had a son, David, with his English housekeeper; after she left him he married his new Russian housekeeper, Valentina Brodsky, known as Vava. They settled on the French Riviera.

Always clowning, with a walk that was more like a bounce, Chagall reminded people of comic actors Charlie Chaplin or Harpo Marx. His cavorting created scenes in restaurants, and neighbors could always hear laughter coming out of his house. (One of his neighbors, a member of the rock band the Rolling Stones, came over and took enough pictures for a whole book of photos of Chagall.) He wore floppy pants and smocks or checked shirts and velvet jackets. He was not a pet person, having been badly bitten by a dog as a child, but did have a gray-and-white cat given to him by Matisse, which he named Le Chat de Matisse.

Chagall worked every day of his life up to age ninety-seven, when he had a heart attack and died.

 RTWORKS

In Chagall's paintings fiddlers play on the roof and fish have wings. The titles of some works—*Self-Portrait with Seven Fingers, Headless Woman with a Pail of Milk, Violinist with the World Upside Down*—indicate their dreamy nature. He worked on many of these paintings at the same time, spreading them around his studio, sometimes turning them to the wall for a while to "ripen." He kept at a painting until something in it surprised him—and then he knew it was finished.

The Birthday, showing himself and Bella so weightless with happiness that Chagall floats in the air, was one of the first of his many paintings in which people float. He put a tiny replica of this work into *The Bride's Chair*, done for his daughter's first wedding, as a good-luck wish to her.

Marcel Duchamp

*French-American artist considered a patron saint of
modern art, an influence on almost every
art movement of this century*

MOST IMPORTANT TO Marcel Duchamp was complete artistic and personal freedom; second most important was a sense of humor. Keeping expenses down was his key to preserving his integrity, and he vowed never to marry, have children, or live lavishly. With his modest inheritance, he invested in sculptures by Rumanian sculptor Constantin Brancusi; if he ran out of money, he would sell a piece.

Fame could certainly interfere with freedom; when Duchamp arrived in the United States from France he was greeted by crowds of reporters. Still, believing he would have more freedom in America than in France, he took a New York City apartment for twenty-five years. Up on the fourth floor, where the rent was twenty-five dollars a month, his furnishings were sparse: a chair, a packing crate to use as another chair, a bed in the corner, and a table with a chessboard always set up. He did not have a phone. He kept a green cardboard box — in it he put scraps of paper on which he'd written down new ideas. Two nails, one with a piece of string hanging down, served as art on the otherwise bare walls. He deliberately accumulated dust to use in his art, so the dust in his apartment was two inches thick.

Duchamp ate downstairs at an Italian restaurant, where he always ordered the same thing: plain spaghetti with butter and Parmesan cheese. Charming and unpretentious, he was elegant in suede shoes and corduroy pant (he liked the sound they made when he walked) and always seemed to be silently laughing.

In 1923, in a decision that astounded the art world, Duchamp announced his "retirement" from art (though he went back to it later without telling anyone). Even when he was offered ten thousand dollars a year to paint a single picture, he refused. He wanted to be a "breather"—one who made an art of living and breathing.

Fascinated by games of chance, he first perfected a system of winning at roulette at Monte Carlo. Then he threw himself into chess, which he played day and night. He went from amateur to professional, "exhibiting" himself in tournaments, and four times was a member of the French team at the International Chess Olympiads. Even in chess, however, he was more interested in making a beautiful work of art than in anything else (like winning), and he was known as an eccentric player.

After keeping company for many years with Mary Reynolds, a wealthy

American widow, Duchamp suddenly married a young French automobile heiress. His friends were speechless. He spent the first week of marriage playing chess so incessantly that one night his wife got up and glued the chess pieces to the board. Four months later they were divorced. At age sixty-seven he married the ex-wife of Pierre Matisse—Alexina Sattler, known as Teeny. Meanwhile, the less he did in the art world, the more attention he got, and late in life his art made him rich. His influence spread to the extent that some say all art being created today is related to ideas he developed.

One night after dinner out with friends, Duchamp told Teeny about something funny he was reading; he laughed, and then his heart stopped beating. He was eighty-one. On his gravestone is inscribed: "Besides, it is always the others who die."

$\mathscr{A}$RTWORKS

 In the first appearance of *Nude Descending a Staircase, No. 2* at a Paris gallery, the nearly unrecognizable figure caused a furor. The other artists exhibiting at the gallery, suspecting that Duchamp was making fun of them, had his two brothers, formally dressed, pay him a call and suggest that he withdraw the work. Duchamp immediately brought the painting home in a taxi. When it was shown later at the notorious New York Armory Show of modern art in 1913, it drew scathing reviews— and huge crowds. It has been called the single most influential painting of the century.

The ready-mades were practical objects Duchamp turned into works of art by signing them. *Hat Rack* was a hat rack and *In Advance of the Broken Arm* was a snow shovel. *Unhappy Ready-made* was a math book hanging from a balcony, so that its equations were exposed to "the facts of life." The most famous ready-made was a reproduction of Leonardo's *Mona Lisa,* to which Duchamp added a mustache and goatee—his way of updating a sacred work of art.

Georgia O'Keeffe

BORN IN SUN PRAIRIE, WISCONSIN, 1887
DIED IN SANTA FE, NEW MEXICO, 1986

*Prominent American painter, known for
images of flowers and desert scenes*

"I AM GOING to be an artist!" Georgia O'Keeffe told a friend at age twelve. She reached her goal by way of teaching art in Amarillo, Texas, and other places in the Wild West. When she wasn't drawing, she coped with shoot-outs, tornadoes, prairie fires, and families that clubbed wild rabbits to death for sport. She seemed to fear nothing, though once she admitted, "I'm frightened all the time. But I've never let it stop me."

Against O'Keeffe's wishes, a friend in New York showed her work to photographer Alfred Stieglitz, the central figure in introducing modern artists in the United States. Despite their many differences, they were married eight years later. He was a city person who craved an audience; she was a country person who found people difficult. She wanted children, but he felt they would divert her from painting and that, at twenty-three years her senior, he was too old. Mutual respect united them—he loved her art ("At last, a woman on paper!"), and she took pleasure in the more than three hundred photographs he took of her (though they created a scandal in some circles).

They lived thirty stories up, on the highest floor of a skyscraper called the Shelton, where they had no curtains to conceal their Manhattan panorama. A solemn couple dressed in look-alike black capes, they often ate at Joe's Spaghetti Restaurant or the Far East Tea Garden. Dignified and direct, O'Keeffe almost always wore black.

O'Keeffe eventually began to spend summers alone in New Mexico, which she adored for its remoteness and scenery. After Stieglitz died she moved there permanently at age fifty-nine and bought Rancho de los Burros, a U-shaped adobe house overlooking dramatic cliffs. When she wasn't painting, she was often rafting on the Colorado River, attending local Indian ceremonies, killing rattlesnakes (she chopped off their heads with a hoe), taking moonlight horseback rides, and lying on her roof in a sleeping bag to savor the view. When she couldn't sleep, she would scrub floors, bake bread, or read cookbooks. She ate homemade yogurt and fried bananas and was especially fond of garlic, raw onions, and hot chiles.

Visitors thought they had never seen anyone happier with life, but local townspeople were suspicious of her. "*Nobody* calls me girlie," O'Keeffe said of one neighbor who made that mistake. Some thought she was a witch—they speculated about the rich outsider, all in black, never smiling, with ferocious chow dogs (Bobo and Chia), not to mention all those

skulls she collected on her hikes. Cowboys warned strangers to steer clear of O'Keeffe's property, adding that she had a shotgun. But many locals appreciated her financial help in the community—supporting such causes as Little League teams, a new recreation center, and a new elementary school.

During the last thirteen years of her life, O'Keeffe's companion was Juan Hamilton, a man in his late twenties who worked for her full time. She began to wear colors in public—turquoise, dark green, maroon. Neighbors spread rumors that the pair was secretly married, but the gossip only amused O'Keeffe. She died peacefully of complications of old age at age ninety-eight. The next day her ashes were scattered over the desert landscape. Her will left the ranch and many paintings to Juan, "my friend."

ARTWORKS

 O'Keeffe painted hundreds of flowers in every shape, color, and size; to her, flowers were a respite from city life. When a series of paintings of calla lilies sold for the highest sum ever paid to a living American artist, it gave her lifetime financial security; she was so dazed she fled to Maine for a month.

 *Cow's Skull: Red, White, and Blue* featured another of O'Keeffe's main subjects—bleached animal bones. She thought of bones as lively, not connected with death. In *Horse's Skull with Pink Rose* she combined flowers and bones. One day she hastily stuck a fabric flower in a skull's eye socket on her way to answer the door—and later liked the effect enough to re-create it on canvas.

 *Summer Days* was one of her favorites and the painting she used for the cover of a book about her work. When a museum hesitated at the four hundred thousand-dollar price she asked, she sold the painting to designer Calvin Klein for one million dollars.

William H. Johnson

*Modern American artist most famous for highly original
treatments of subjects from African-American life*

"IN THE ARTISTIC realm," William H. Johnson once said, "race ultimately isn't very important."

Part African American, part white, and part Sioux Indian, Johnson had found that race was *all*-important in the small, strictly segregated town where he grew up. With an uncle's help, he saved enough money from odd jobs at the YMCA and the railroad station to get himself out of South Carolina to art school in New York at age seventeen. Money from scholarships and work as a short-order cook and hotel porter got him even farther — to Paris. After this Johnson mostly lived abroad, where he felt there was more acceptance of blacks, and for the sake of his career, even his teachers encouraged him to stay there.

Marriage to Holcha Krake, a Danish weaver and textile expert who was sixteen years older than he, kept Johnson based in Denmark. Despite their different ages and backgrounds, they were devoted to each other. She encouraged his work, arranged joint exhibitions of her weaving and his paintings, and supported them with her sales.

Johnson was a familiar sight around the fishing village of Kerteminde, with his portable easel balanced on his head, rolled-up canvases under his arm, and his pipe in his mouth. He wore the same blue shirts Danish workers did, with wide cotton pants, strong sandals, and a bandanna around his neck. He attracted audiences that appreciated the graceful and rhythmic way he danced while he painted. When he was not working he jogged and did handstands on the beach, helped fishermen bring in the day's catch (though extreme seasickness kept him off their boats), and played geography guessing games with local kids. On rainy days he took outdoor showers by wrapping a towel around himself and stepping outside. He and Holcha traveled as much as they could, backpacking and bicycling throughout Europe and North Africa.

Johnson could sometimes seem mysterious—brooding, unusually reserved, and solemn. Fellow artist and friend Romare Bearden described him as "rather serious." He was known to lose his temper at times, especially if anyone messed up his clean and orderly studio. Once when he was hit by a stray snowball, he chased the Danish boy who threw it all the way into his schoolroom and demanded an apology. He was not an easy person to get along with—he could silence people with a look—and for the most part he liked to keep to himself.

After his beloved Holcha died of breast cancer, Johnson talked of nothing else but her. He grew moodier, more irritable, and, his anxious

friends noticed, emotionally disturbed. He began living on the street even though, always careful with money, he had enough saved up to stay in hotels. When he was occasionally arrested for vagrancy, he could pull out a thousand-dollar bill and get himself released.

Less than three years after Holcha's death, Johnson was diagnosed with disabling brain damage from syphilis and sent to live in a mental hospital in New York. Unlike Van Gogh, Johnson was unable to paint while he was hospitalized and was shocked when people suggested it. He never painted again. Twenty-three years later, at age sixty-nine, he died of pancreatitis. That year his work was included in several exhibitions in the United States, and his reputation has grown ever since.

ARTWORKS

Interested in all aspects of blacks in history, Johnson depicted quiet rural scenes (as in *Going to Church*, perhaps his most famous work) as well as energetic street life (as in *Café* and *Street Musicians*) and events like the 1943 Harlem riots and the daily lives of blacks fighting in segregated World War II units. Sometimes he signed his work Mahlinda, a more African-sounding name.

Johnson got just enough public recognition to keep him going — *Chain Gang*, for example, was exhibited at the New York World's Fair of 1940 — but during his life European art was all the rage. By the time collectors were noticing American artists, most of Johnson's work was stored in a warehouse. In 1955 his paintings narrowly escaped destruction when his savings (which were paying the storage fees) ran out.

HOW TO SHOCK THE WORLD
EVERY TWENTY-FOUR HOURS
Salvador Dali

BORN IN 1904 AND DIED IN 1989 IN FIGUERAS, SPAIN

*Flamboyant Spanish painter famous for putting his
dreams and nightmares into realistic paintings*

"NOTHING IS MORE important to Me than Me," Salvador Dali wrote, and with his glittering stare and fits of mad laughter, he dedicated his life to proving his genius. He was frequently expelled from school, once for telling three professors he knew more about art than all of them put together.

Gala, a much older Russian woman whose real name was Helena and who was married to someone else, decided to dedicate her life to Dali as well and became his sole model and assistant. He liked her because she changed clothes three times a day; at each meeting he discovered her anew. After her divorce and their marriage, they lived in poverty at first but, dreading the neighbors' pity, left large tips in restaurants. Later, when his paintings were selling for one million dollars each and he was eating oysters with princes, Dali made sure his old friends—still living on sardines and bread crusts—knew it.

Dali did not excel at ordinary life. He was notorious for not knowing how to count money; the only transportation that didn't petrify him was a taxi; and he was afraid to expose his feet—a problem when he went shopping for shoes. To ward off evil spirits he carried a special piece of driftwood, but nevertheless his fears increased. He was afraid of germs, assassination (he had his chauffeur taste his food), and especially grasshoppers, which so terrified him that he never walked on grass. When traveling, he was known to attach his canvases to his body with strings, for fear of theft.

Dali lived life like an animated Dali painting, explaining, "The only difference between Dali and a crazy man is that Dali is not crazy." He wore his mustache in the exaggerated style of his idol, the Spanish artist Velazquez, waxing the ends to hold the curl. He would leap into the air to get himself noticed and once drove around in a white Rolls-Royce filled to the roof with cauliflower. When he attended a party where guests were to dress up as their dreams, he came as a decomposing corpse. To greet reporters who met his ship, he persuaded the ship's baker to make him an eight-foot-long loaf of French bread he could wave about.

No amount of publicity was too much. Shortly after landing on the cover of *Time* magazine, Dali was arrested for smashing the window of a department store that had dared to change a display he had designed. Another day he donned a deep-sea diving suit before giving a lecture. Not only was the heavy helmet soundproof—no one could hear him—but no one noticed he was suffocating. The audience, roaring with laughter,

thought his gestures for help were meant to be funny, and not until he almost fainted was he rescued. If he was accused of going too far, Dali would reply, "It's the only place I ever wanted to go," or else say with a sigh, "It's very difficult to shock the world every twenty-four hours."

He wintered in New York, where he would dine on duck liver and raisins with thirty of his closest friends (preferably beautiful ones) and one or two ocelots (declawed). He summered at a fisherman's hut in Spain, where a stuffed polar bear at the door held umbrellas and where meals were simple—fresh fish and salads of tomatoes. Eventually Gala moved to an eleventh-century castle Dali had lovingly restored for her, where he was allowed to visit only if he asked her in advance in writing. He moved in on the night she died, entombed her in the castle crypt, and prepared his grave next to hers. He lived his last seven years in the castle as a recluse, taken care of by his manservant, Arturo, and four round-the-clock nurses.

"Geniuses must never die," he promised, but in fact he did, at age eighty-four.

ARTWORKS

🎨 One night Dali, pleading a headache, backed out of going to the movies with Gala and friends. He sat for a long time at the dinner table, staring at the melting Camembert cheese. Before he went to bed, he took a last look at a landscape he was working on—and suddenly added three melting watches, thus creating *The Persistence of Memory*, probably his most famous painting.

🎨 *Daddy Longlegs of the Evening . . . Hope!*, Dali's first work to sell to the Morse family of St. Petersburg, Florida, sold so early in his career that the frame cost more than the painting. Dali's paintings were thought scandalous by the Morses' friends, but the family ended up buying one-fourth of Dali's entire output and established a Dali museum. They even published the *Dali Primer*, a guide to the way he spoke English, which was so eccentric that not even English-speakers could understand it.

A Tiger on the Stairway
Isamu Noguchi

BORN IN LOS ANGELES, CALIFORNIA, 1904
DIED IN NEW YORK CITY, 1988

Japanese-American sculptor whose work is in museums
all over the world — and, as public art, in
parks, gardens, and playgrounds

WITH HIS MIXED heritage — half Japanese, half American (Scottish, Irish, and American Indian) — Isamu Noguchi felt out of place wherever he was. In Japan he was considered not Japanese enough; in America he was not American enough. Even in the art world he wasn't necessarily welcomed — art teachers advised him to take up medicine, and while he was completing his first public art in Mexico City, his relationship with the artist Frida Kahlo caused Diego Rivera, her husband, to threaten him with a gun.

But nothing ever crushed what Noguchi called his "love affair with stone" — not even years of vehement opposition to making his sculpture ideas real. Park commissioners and administrators, whose approval he needed, occasionally lacked his vision or deferred to neighbors who complained about living near a controversial sculpture. Noguchi found the endless petty disputes very upsetting.

What affected him even more deeply were events between Japan and the United States. During World War II he voluntarily committed himself to a Japanese internment camp in the Arizona desert, hoping to design parks and playgrounds for the uprooted residents. After the United States

dropped atom bombs on Japan, killing relatives in his father's family, he stopped working for two years.

Restless, Noguchi spent much of his time traveling, hunting around the world for the best stone and journeying between his two worlds. In Long Island City, not far from Manhattan, an ugly factory building concealed his spacious and elegant living and working quarters. High above his studio and home in the mountain forest of Skikoku, Japan, was a temple he visited, joining pilgrims who were dressed all in white. One of the few furnishings in his two hundred-year-old house was a large xylophone from Indonesia.

When Noguchi married a famous Japanese actress, Yoshiko Yamaguchi, their formal wedding in full Japanese dress was broadcast by radio throughout Japan. Noguchi began to wear traditional kimonos, as well as beautiful but uncomfortable straw sandals, and insisted that his wife wear them, too. They were divorced four years later.

Noguchi could be ill-at-ease, even short-tempered. Some friends thought he was selfish, and even he called the stone he worked with "a reflection of my rocky heart." One of his few close friends was American architect R. Buckminster Fuller, with whom he would walk and talk all over

New York, stopping for countless cups of coffee at a cafe called Romany Marie's. Nothing made Noguchi angrier than having his artwork altered. He would kick away shrubs if they hid his sculptures, and he once accused a bank of vandalism when it took apart one of his works after receiving complaints that the piece was unsafe.

Full of energy, Noguchi walked fast and took stairways like a tiger. Some things made him impatient—when a taxi stalled, he'd get out and walk, and if a clerk was too slow, he'd decide not to buy the item. Even after he developed a back injury when he was in his seventies, he still climbed mountains to hunt for stone. At his eightieth birthday party he danced for hours. Indeed, when Noguchi died four years later of heart failure, the main reaction of his friends was surprise.

ARTWORKS

Noguchi's most ambitious work was a fountain for the Detroit Civic Center Plaza, a spectacular stainless steel structure with thirty-five different light and water configurations. Noguchi took on the project because he wanted to help a city troubled by the 1960s racial riots.

Noguchi considered many things a form of sculpture: gardens, buildings, cemeteries, furniture, even theater (sculpture come to life). To many people he is best known for his invention of paper lanterns known as *akari* lamps (he thought of them as light sculptures). They were first made by lantern makers in Gifu, Japan, after Noguchi asked the mayor what he could do to help the town's economy.

After thirty years of rejection of his ideas for playgrounds, Noguchi finally completed *Playscapes,* in Atlanta, Georgia. A colorful wraparound sculpture garden for children, it contains swings, slides, jungle gyms, and sandboxes.

Diego Rivera &
Frida Kahlo

BORN IN 1886 IN GUANAJUATO, MEXICO, AND
DIED IN 1957 IN MEXICO CITY, MEXICO (RIVERA)
BORN IN 1907 AND DIED IN 1954 IN COYOACAN, MEXICO (KAHLO)

*Distinguished Mexican muralist and distinctive Mexican painter
stormily married to each other*

WHEN DIEGO RIVERA and Frida Kahlo were married, he was forty-two and on his third marriage; she was twenty-two and the marriage was her first. He was a national monument; she was teaching herself to paint. And there were plenty of other differences between them.

He weighed three hundred pounds and was more than six feet tall, so large that he couldn't find underwear to fit (she had it made for him, in bright pink cotton). She was ninety-eight pounds and five feet three inches. People called them the Elephant and the Dove.

Rivera was someone to lean on, with the energy of ten men, capable of working for days at a time. Kahlo was fragile. Childhood polio had caused one of her legs to stop growing, and at age eighteen she suffered severe injuries when she was pierced by an iron handrail in a horrific bus accident. She went on to endure thirty-two operations in attempts to relieve the pain. She couldn't paint for more than an hour at a time and was often bedridden.

Rivera's art covered entire buildings and dealt encyclopedically with the land and people of Mexico. Kahlo's paintings were small—some the size of this book—and most were deeply personal.

Rivera was a messy dresser. He wore baggy overalls (usually paint-smeared), big black shoes, a Stetson hat, and he often carried a large pistol. Kahlo took such exquisite care with her clothes, no matter how she was feeling, that people called her the Walking Flower. She wore elaborate blouses, long skirts of purple or red velvet, and layers of petticoats she embroidered with Mexican sayings. She pulled her hair back tightly, embellishing it with clips, combs, and fresh blossoms. Sometimes she wore so much jewelry—she was known to wear twenty rings at once—that she clanked when she moved.

He ate a lot (Kahlo would bring him big lunches in baskets covered with flowers and love notes), while she was a picky eater. She could think of only three American foods she liked: malted milk, applesauce, and American cheese.

Rivera could be generous but frequently was unreliable, too absorbed in his work to take much interest in people or money—sometimes he left large checks lying around for years before he cashed them. Kahlo was thoughtful and could listen to people for hours, always wanting to hear someone's life story. She kept scrupulous accounts of her money.

At fifteen Kahlo had told friends that her ambition was to have children with the famous Diego Rivera. By the time they married, he didn't want more than the several children he already had, and after numerous miscarriages, Kahlo sadly accepted that she was too frail to have children.

For all their differences, what kept Kahlo and Rivera together?

Both loved to laugh. She had a contagious belly laugh and once wrote, "Nothing is worth more than *laughter*." She tried whenever possible to deal with her pain by using humor. Rivera was known as a hugely entertaining teller of tall tales and made-up stories about himself. At parties the two of them made friends laugh by pouring powdered sugar all over a table and creating cityscapes.

Both were concerned about improving their country's government. Rivera believed that art could transform society and that murals were the best way for ordinary people to see art. Kahlo joined him in marches and other efforts for social change.

They both had strong opinions—and so had many fights, separations,

and reconciliations. Each also had many affairs, but they always came back to one another—each was the central figure in the other's life. When Kahlo was in the hospital, Rivera would rock her to sleep or entertain her by pretending to be a circus bear dancing around her bed with a tambourine. She signed her letters to him with magenta-pink lipstick kisses and did everything she could to make him happy.

Both drew crowds. Rivera at work was considered a must-see tourist attraction; people would buy tickets just to watch him paint. Kahlo and her outfits could stop traffic; parades of children would follow her. Together they were a sensation—he presented himself like a king; she carried herself like a queen. When they entered a theater, people looked at them instead of at the performers on stage. Details of their colorful, glamorous life were written up in the papers, and people the world over addressed them by their first names.

Both were childlike and easily bored with anything except themselves and each other. He preferred her to bathe him (otherwise he wouldn't bathe) and demanded lots of bath toys. She had an enormous collection of dolls (whenever friends left on a trip, she would request, "Bring me a doll") and pets, including spider monkeys, turkeys, and parrots. One parrot named Bonito slept under the covers with her.

They liked each other's looks. Rivera admired Kahlo's eyebrows, which met in the middle, and her mustache—he was furious once when she shaved it off. During especially bitter quarrels, she would wound him by cutting off her long hair. She teasingly called him Frog-Face and Fatbelly, but in truth she adored his Buddha-like appearance.

Above all they respected each other's art. Kahlo thought Rivera was the greatest artist in the world and defended him verbally and even physically—she once jumped between him and a man with a gun. When Picasso asserted that no one could paint like Kahlo, Rivera agreed. "We are all clods next to Frida," Rivera said, and he did all he could to encourage her. Both were successful. Critics lionized him, and she had no trouble selling every work she painted.

They lived in Mexico City in two separate houses linked by a bridge. Her house was blue; his house was pink. Concerned over neighbors' approval of their guests, they simply bought the lot next door to put more distance between themselves and their neighbors. After a long breakfast together, he would disappear to work and she would go to her studio, to Tarzan movies (or the Three Stooges or the Marx Brothers) or to boxing matches. At night they met for late suppers of hot chocolate and sweet rolls.

Less than a year before she died at age forty-seven, Kahlo made herself part of an exhibit of her work. Too ill to leave her huge four-poster bed, she had the bed moved to the gallery, where friends sang songs to her. The last words she wrote in her diary were: "I hope the exit is joyful—and I hope never to come back." After her death friends reported that Rivera became "an old man in a few hours." He soon remarried but died at age seventy-one, within three years of his marriage, after a stroke.

RTWORKS

Rivera painted more than two and a half miles of murals in his lifetime. The first was a series of 124 panels encompassing the entire history of Mexico. It took him more than four years, working eight to fifteen hours at a stretch, to do all the painting by hand. Upon completing the work he was instantly famous.

Rivera's murals—which always sparked controversy—were vulnerable to attack by mutilation or acid throwing. The most vigorous protest came when Rivera (a "foreigner") worked inside New York City's Radio City Music Hall; his murals were destroyed before he could finish.

The Two Fridas, probably Kahlo's most famous work, was painted during a painful separation from Rivera; they divorced and remarried the next year. Most of her work was autobiographical; when she was bedridden it was convenient, with mirror in hand, to paint herself. Those who didn't find her work shockingly personal valued it highly. *Diego and I* became the first Latin American painting to sell for more than one million dollars; rock star Madonna owns *Self-Portrait with Monkey* and other Kahlo works.

In *Frida and Diego Rivera,* the painting Kahlo did for their wedding, he holds his palette and brushes more tightly than he holds her hand, her way of showing that with him art came first. She holds no art supplies, to show that she valued him even more than her art.

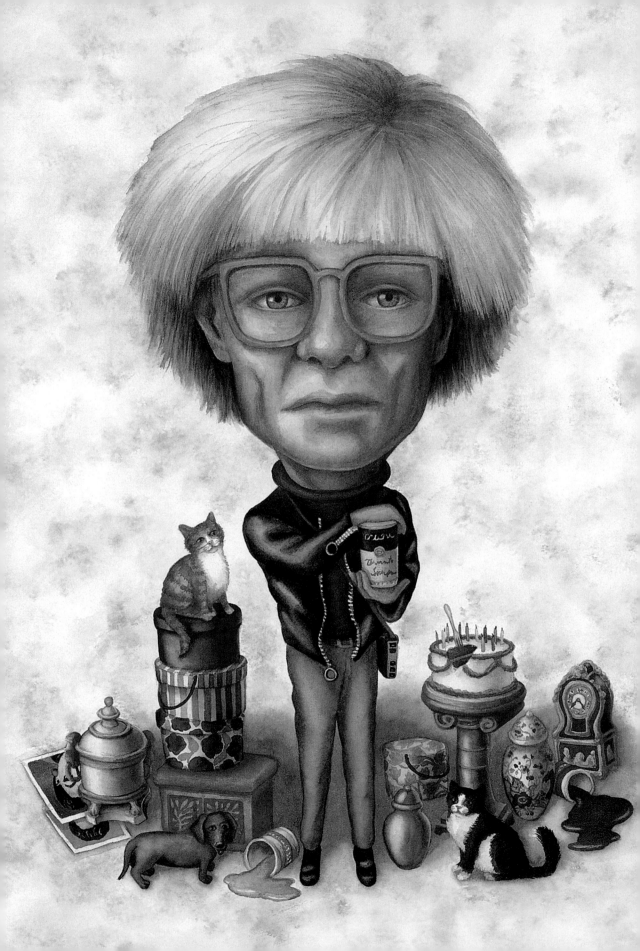

EATING THE ENTIRE BIRTHDAY CAKE
ANDY WARHOL

BORN IN PITTSBURGH, PENNSYLVANIA, 1928
DIED IN NEW YORK CITY, 1987

*Contemporary American artist, famous
for repetitive images and portraits*

ANDREW WARHOLA GREW up as a sickly child in Pittsburgh, Pennsylvania, where his mother gave him a Hershey bar every time he finished a page in his coloring book. Later, attracted by the excitement of New York City, he became a fashion illustrator for such magazines as *Seventeen* and *Glamour* and was known as the best shoe illustrator in New York. Magazines misprinted his name as Warhol.

His first apartments in New York, shared with his mother, were usually infested with roaches, with no hot water and the bathtub in the kitchen. They kept between eight and twenty cats at a time, the smell of which sometimes overpowered the scent of Warhol's paints.

Warhol decided early on that a bizarre personal image would lead to sales. The first time he showed his art to potential collectors, he opened his door wearing an eighteenth-century mask of jewels and feathers, with the same rock song blasting over and over (he had a habit of listening to a song one hundred times in a row). Eventually his trademark look consisted of sunglasses (which got bigger as he aged), blond wigs (which got bushier), black leather jackets, and high-heeled boots. The only people who ever saw him without his wig were his young nephews, who idolized Uncle Andy because he always kept them sup-plied with crayons. He emphasized his extreme pallor with makeup. He seemed frail and unearthly, but he did one hundred push-ups and fifty pull-ups almost every morning.

Warhol worked twelve hours a day at his studio (known as the Fac-tory), then went out to parties (up to twenty a night) until 3:00 or 4:00 A.M., surrounded by an entourage of colorful people. His nickname was Drella (a combination of Dracula and Cinderella). At times he lived on candy and pastries, and for a treat would buy himself a whole birthday cake to eat. At other times he was more health conscious, favoring bean sand-wiches, vegetable puree, and raw garlic.

Though he was frequently inarticulate in public (favorite expressions were "gee," "wow," and "uh"), Warhol became perhaps the most quoted artist in the world, with such statements as "In the future everyone will be famous for fifteen minutes." He called the telephone his best friend and carried a tape recorder in order to record hours of his conversations (he adored gossip) every day.

Warhol never married. As a homosexual in conservative society, he kept his sexual orientation secret until after he was rich and famous. After his mother died he lived alone—except for two maids, Nena and Au-rora, and two miniature dachshunds, Archie and Amos—in a five-story

townhouse filled with valuable antiques, artwork, and his amazing collections (such as 175 cookie jars). Every room except the kitchen was a storeroom — even the bedroom had green boxes of wigs stacked near the TV set. He had four hundred wigs in all.

Warhol thought of dying as "the most embarrassing thing that can ever happen to you." He nearly died after being shot in the stomach by the founder of an organization called SCUM (Society for Cutting Up Men) but lived another eighteen years, dying at age fifty-eight after routine gall bladder surgery. Two thousand people attended his memorial service; six thousand came to the auction of his collections. His will left the bulk of his more than one hundred million-dollar estate to charity, most to a foundation to be set up "for the advancement of the visual arts." The Andy Warhol Museum, the largest museum in the United States devoted to a single artist, opened in Pittsburgh in 1994.

ARTWORKS

Warhol's most famous and most valuable images were his paintings of cans for each of the thirty-two varieties of Campbell's soup. Although many deep meanings have been attributed to them, in fact Warhol just loved soup (especially tomato), which his mother had often made for him when they were poor. "I paint things I always thought beautiful — things you use every day and never think about," he once said.

Warhol was famous for doing portraits of people he had never met — up until his time, artists had done self-portraits, hired models, or worked on commissioned portraits. After actress Marilyn Monroe's suicide in 1962 — on the day his exhibit called *Soup Cans* closed — he decided to paint *Marilyn*, a portrait of an American symbol. It was the first of his celebrity paintings and an example of his fascination with the idea of fame.

ARTISTIC TERMS

canvas	a cloth surface on which paintings are made
commission	a formal paid assignment to complete a work of art
dealer	one who sells art on behalf of the artist
easel	a stand that supports an artist's canvas
exhibition	a public showing of works of art
landscape	a picture that depicts natural inland scenery
miniature	a very small painting
model	someone hired or asked to pose for an artist
mural	large artwork that is applied to the surface of a wall or ceiling
painting	a work produced through the art of applying paint
palette	a smooth surface on which an artist mixes paints
patron	an influential or wealthy supporter of an artist
portrait	an artistic representation of a person, usually emphasizing the face
print	a work of art intended for reproduction under the artist's supervision
public art	art exposed to general view, often in parks and plazas
Renaissance	transitional period of European history between medieval and modern times, marked by a flowering of the arts
retrospective	an exhibition of works spanning part or all of an artist's career
sculpture	a three-dimensional work of art
self-portrait	a portrait of an artist done by himself or herself
sketch	a rough drawing
still life	a work of art that depicts inanimate objects arranged by the artist

$\mathcal{I}$NDEX OF $\mathcal{A}$RTISTS

FOR FURTHER READING . . . AND LOOKING

Alexander, Sidney. *Marc Chagall: An Intimate Biography*. New York: Paragon House, 1989.

Ashton, Dore. *Noguchi East and West*. New York: Knopf, 1992.

Bockris, Victor. *The Life and Death of Andy Warhol*. New York: Bantam Books, 1989.

Bramly, Serge. *Leonardo: Discovering the Life of Leonardo da Vinci*. New York: HarperCollins, 1991.

Hale, Nancy. *Mary Cassatt*. Reading, Mass.: Addison-Wesley, 1987.

Herrera, Hayden. *Frida: A Biography of Frida Kahlo*. New York: Harper & Row, 1983.

___ . *Matisse: A Portrait*. New York: Harcourt Brace, 1993.

Huffington, Arianna Stassinopoulos. *Picasso: Creator and Destroyer*. New York: Simon & Schuster, 1988.

Kearns, Martha. *Käthe Kollwitz: Woman and Artist*. New York: The Feminist Press, 1976.

Klein, H. Arthur, and Mina C. Klein. *Peter Bruegel the Elder: Artist of Abundance*. New York: Macmillan, 1968.

Lane, Richard. *Hokusai: Life and Work*. New York: Dutton, 1989.

Lisle, Laurie. *Portrait of an Artist: A Biography of Georgia O'Keeffe*. New York: Washington Square Press, 1986.

McLanathan, Richard. *Michelangelo*. New York: Abrams, 1993.

Mee, Charles L., Jr. *Rembrandt's Portrait: A Biography*. New York: Simon & Schuster, 1988.

Perlingieri, Ilya Sandra. *Sofonisba Anguissola: The First Great Woman Artist of the Renaissance*. New York: Rizzoli, 1992.

Powell, Richard J. *Homecoming: The Art and Life of William H. Johnson*. New York: Rizzoli, 1991.

Secrest, Meryle. *Salvador Dali*. New York: Dutton, 1986.

Sweetman, David. *Van Gogh: His Life and His Art*. New York: Simon & Schuster, 1990.

Tomkins, Calvin, and the editors of Time-Life Books. *The World of Marcel Duchamp*. New York: Time Incorporated, 1966.

Wolfe, Bertram D. *The Fabulous Life of Diego Rivera*. Lanham, Md.: Scarborough House, 1990.

. . . and works of art by the artists in this book.